The 21 Day Debt Revolution

Jonathan Alexander Scott

Copyright © 2014 J.A.Scott Publications

All rights reserved.

ISBN: 1505644534
ISBN-13: 978-1505644531

DEDICATION

To my wife and children, who have stuck by me through thick and thin.
I love you.

CONTENTS

Introduction	1
A challenge	4
Day 1. Goal Setting (Phase 1)	6
Day 2. Goal Setting	12
Day 3. Reversal	18
Day 4. The Emergency Fund	22
Day 5. Making Your money Count	25
Day 6. New Spending Habits	29
Day 7. Family	32
Day 8. Snowball	34
Day 9. Minimise Expenditure	38
Day 10. Future Planning	41
Day 11. Cars	44
Day 12. Get the Family Involved	48
Day 13. Review Day	50
Day 14. A day for family & friends	53
Day 15. Ebay	55
Day 16. Maximise Income	57
Day 17. Travel	61
Day 18. Career Dreams and Aspirations	64
Day 19. All about you	68
Day 20. Weekly Review	71
Day 21. The End	73
Day 22. The Future Begins	75
About the Author	81
Disclaimer	82

ACKNOWLEDGMENTS

Thank you to Peter Bangs and Becky Boxall who read this book long before it was ready to be published and helped ensure that my many mistakes and strange turns of phrase were ironed out. Guys, this would not have been possible without you both.

INTRODUCTION

Like you, I have also been in debt.

A lot of debt. At my lowest point I owed over £30,000 (approximately $48,000) to various banks and credit cards.

With a wife and young children to feed, this was a heavy burden to carry. I'd regularly wake up at night with cold sweats, worrying about how I was going to get through the month. I'd worry about how I was going to pay the bills and still have money to feed my children.

The worst thing was that, to everyone else, I appeared to be absolutely fine. I lived behind a facade of cheerful calm. I was easy going, I'd go out to restaurants, buy the latest music, go on holiday...

I was doing everything a "normal" person is expected to do.

My job was well paid and very secure, earning about £35,000 ($56,000) a year, which is higher than the average salary here in the UK. We ran two cars, I had the latest smart phone, tablet and laptop.

My wife and I had all the appearances of a successful, hardworking member of society and yet, I felt trapped.

I felt hemmed in by my mounting debt, by that cold sinking feeling when I had to check my bank balance.

The fear that I would be faced with that dreaded message: *"There are insufficient funds to complete your request."*

I used to love hearing the sound of the ATM whirring to life, a clear indication that actually, this time, it would give me the money I had requested. The relief was always short lived, though, quickly replaced by the guilt of knowing that I couldn't really afford to spend that money, that I really should have made some sandwiches at home rather than buying lunch out. Again.

The arguments at home over money led me to a place where at times I wondered whether my marriage was going to survive. We eventually arrived at a place where we just didn't talk about it.

Our finances became a taboo subject as it seemed easier to ignore them than fight through to a solution.

Unsurprisingly, not talking did not solve the problem and our debts continued to mount.

I eventually spoke to a friend of mine about the problem. This really was the turning point as he offered me hope where before I could see none.

He told me that all I needed was a simple plan and he suggested that maybe I needed to try to learn about managing finances so that I could come up with a plan that would work for me.

So I did.

I researched and read, book after book. I went to online forums on money saving and debt reduction.

Some places offered great advice and others *not* so great (I would never recommend "Stoozing", i.e. "flipping" 0% credit cards to make money to pay off debt. That's a recipe for disaster!)

After a lot of research (and much trial and error), I was able to devise a plan that worked for me.

A simple plan that will work for you too, if you follow it.

Don't misunderstand me though, just because it's simple, doesn't mean it's easy. You will need to put in some hard work and make some sacrifices but there is a saying that I truly believe:

Victory without sacrifice is no victory at all.

Over the following chapters I want to share this plan with you and show you how, over the next 21 days, you can change your lifestyle and put you and your family on the road to a debt free, more peaceful, life.

I want you to know that you are not alone and that I know exactly how you feel.

I also want to promise you this:

There is a way out.

There is hope.

You can escape the stranglehold of debt and live a life that is free from the constant worry, the nagging voices and the permanent state of fear.

You too can live a life of financial freedom.

A CHALLENGE

This book could change your life.

In fact, I challenge you to apply this plan to your finances and stick with it.

Then watch as your debt reduces, your savings increase and your quality of life skyrockets.

This will only happen when you make your financial future the top priority in your life.

Every decision you make about money must be measured against whether it will bring you closer or further away from your goal.

Don't worry, I will cover goal setting and how to maintain motivation in a future chapter, but I need you to promise that you will do everything in your power to achieve your aim.

Twenty-one days is how long it takes to create a new habit, so complete the daily exercises for the next few weeks and marvel at how much your life will change.

You may even discover that your relationship with your partner improves, or that the added discipline of following this plan helps you to achieve other goals in your life.

You could lose that weight you've been trying to lose for years.

You could finally start that business you've always dreamed of.

You might learn to play an instrument.

Anything is possible when you set your mind to it, and as you start reaching goals in one area, you quickly see that this momentum carries through into all other areas of your life.

Accept the challenge.

    Your freedom starts now.

DAY 1. GOAL SETTING (PHASE 1)

Whenever you set off on a journey, it is important to know where you want to go.

I know this is an overused example but it's a great one, so I will use it anyway:

When setting off, unless you tell your sat nav *where* you want to go, it cannot give you directions.

Your sat nav then breaks your journey down into individual segments; *"Turn left at St George's Avenue."*, *"Turn right in 300 yards."*

Each instruction given is a mini goal, a step towards reaching your final destination.

This is the purpose of setting goals.

There are three phases to setting good goals.

The first is working out where you would like to go; You need to define your destination. This is what we will focus on today.

The second is working out where you are right now. (This will be covered in Day Two.)

The third phase is working out what steps need to be taken to move from where you are now to where you need to get. This is exactly what this book is all about.

Together we will take the steps necessary to journey from where you are now to where you need to go.

It won't always be easy but what a great story you'll have to tell when you get there!

Getting Started

So, as I mentioned earlier, it is time to work out where you want your final destination to be.

Your freedom.

We must focus on making this more than just a simple sentence on a piece of paper. This has got to be something that truly resonates with you. Something that gets you fired up.

I need you to know not only where you want to get to but also why you want to get there and what you are willing to do to achieve this.

If you are married, or in a stable long term relationship, I would strongly encourage you to get your partner involved at this stage, on Day 1, so that you take this journey hand-in-hand and work together towards the same goal.

As an aside, I would also encourage you to have a notebook or journal of some description to hand when completing these exercises.

There is something real, permanent and binding about actually putting pen to paper, rather than simply typing on a computer screen.

I find that writing things down actually has a lasting impact on you, focusing your mind and giving resolve where there may not have been much before.

Sign a contract between you and your partner, declaring your intention and your goals. There is a certain level of gravitas that accompanies signing a contract with a pen rather than simply typing your name on a computer screen or entering a PIN code...

Exercise 1

Sit down, with your partner if you have one, and open your notebook.

Now, imagine a life without debt.

A life where your income could be used to pay for what you want rather than to simply service your debts.

What would you do?

What would you spend your money on?

What job would you have?

I am serious. I want you to imagine your perfect life.

Now write it down.

Make what you write more than a simple wish. I.e. don't simply write: *"I want to live in a bigger house."*

Write down something descriptive. Imagine the perfect house (if that is your dream) and describe it fully. Describe its location, how many rooms it will have, how big the garden is going to be.

Everything.

Also, rather than writing *"I want to..."* write *"I will..."*

For example:

"I will live in a big detached house. My house will be in the countryside, close enough to the city so that I can travel in to the shops and see friends easily, but far enough away that I can relax in a peaceful environment, away from the hustle and bustle of busy city life.

My house will be detached with a large garden, big enough for my children to run around in. It will have enough bedrooms for my children not to have to share and it will have a spare room so that we can have guests come and visit.

It will also have a room that can be used as my office, where I can write, read and listen to music without being disturbed..." etc...

This is the sort of thing I want you to write.

If you are in any way artistic, or enjoy craft, you could look through magazines and find pictures of houses, or jobs, or holidays that form part of your dream. Cut them out and stick them in your journal.

Sometimes visual references are a great help at times when motivation is lacking and you need a quick reminder of why you are doing this.

Motivation

Reality is that money does not, in itself, motivate people.

Getting paid does not motivate people to work hard, to dream big or to strive to improve their lives. At most it makes people get out of bed and go to work in the morning but it doesn't *actually motivate* anyone to do a good job.

Motivation comes from elsewhere.

It comes from the people you work with or the satisfaction you gain from completing a task well, or from being able to use skills that only you have.

Motivation comes from being recognised for your achievements and from being able to use your skills to improve your environment, whether that be your home, your work or any other setting.

Money is a tool which can help you achieve these things, but it will never truly motivate you.

Motivation is driven by emotion.

The *joy* of achievement.

The *joy* of being debt free.

That moment of *pure happiness* when your child hugs you and says "Thank you Daddy!" in that genuine, heartfelt way that only a child can.

Even negative emotions can motivate change, however, this journey will be much more enjoyable if we focus on the happiness and freedom at the end of the journey rather than the fear and despair that may have brought us here in the first place.

This leads us on to our next exercise.

Exercise 2

Whatever your dream is, I want you to imagine it vividly. Imagine that moment when you finally achieve it and write down how you will feel when your dream finally becomes a reality.

Again, don't describe simple facts, e.g. "*I will feel happy.*" but rather, describe everything you can imagine.

For example: "*When I take possession of the keys to my new family home and unlock the door, I will be overjoyed. I may not say much, but the way my children run ahead of me, exploring every corner of their new home and shouting with delight at the things they find, will fill my heart with joy.*

I will feel proud and at peace; having been able to provide for my family in a way that previously I never thought would have been possible. There will be no weight on my shoulders and I will feel completely free and at peace..." etc.

Writing down how you feel will focus your reasons for wanting to change your life.

This is where the revolution begins.

From now on, you are no longer simply running away in order to survive.

You are running towards something better.

You are on your way to a life of financial freedom and the peace that accompanies that.

> Rather than just trying to survive, you now have a reason to live!

DAY 2. GOAL SETTING

Today we will really start tackling the challenge that is your debt.

By the end of the day you will be looking out at the journey you are about to embark on and will be ready to take that first step.

Continuing with the Sat Nav metaphor, this is where we identify the starting point of the journey.

There are two things a Sat Nav requires in order to successfully calculate a route:

1. The destination. We covered this in yesterday's tasks. You already know where you want and need to go.

2. The starting point. Without a starting point, a point from which to plan the route, the sat nav is unable to carry out its function.

So today we will determine where you are in relation to your final goal. This is a daunting task and it will force you to face a reality that you may have been avoiding for some time.

Trust me, I know what it's like to avoid checking your credit card bills, to refuse to look at the bank account balance for fear of what we may, or more likely, may not, find.

But don't worry; this is the start of a new day.

It is vitally important, when completing this exercise, that you do not dwell on past mistakes. This is especially true if you are doing this with your partner.

Remember: You cannot change what has happened, you can only learn from it and use these lessons to affect what happens in the future.

This is not the time to start playing any form of blame game. In a relationship, you have both made mistakes and you are *both* responsible for how you got to this point and therefore *both* responsible for changing your current reality and shaping your future.

Departure

It's time to find your starting point, plan your route and begin your journey.

Let's go.

Exercise 1

Sit down with your journal/notebook and get all your statements, bills, account details, etc, in front of you.

If you need to log in to your internet banking, do that.

Now, I want you to create two lists.

The first list is a list of your debts in ascending order (from smallest debt to largest).

All of them.

If you owe a friend, £20 ($30) then list it.

If you owe your parents some money, list this debt.

Everything.

The only caveat is that you should leave out your mortgage. Whilst this is a debt that I would love you to get rid of, it is not one that needs to be tackled first. We should concentrate on getting rid of all other debts before your mortgage.

Trust me on this.

Next, I want you to list the minimum payment for each debt. (This is to make a later exercise easier.)

So, your page should look something like this:

Joe Bloggs (Friend): £40   Minimum Payment: n/a

Parents: £350   Minimum Payment: £25/month

Car Loan: £4597   Minimum Payment: £187/month

Credit Card: £5200   Minimum Payment: £108/month

Bank Loan: £12,390   Minimum Payment: £127/month

Total: £22,577

There is a valid reason for listing the debts in this order, which I will explain in another chapter.

On the opposite page, I want you to show much money you currently have at your disposal.

Your page should look something like this:

Current Account (Joint): £547

Current Account (Partner A): £276

Current Account (Partner B): £124

Savings Account: £690

Total: £1637

The reason for listing how much money you have in your account is twofold:

Firstly, it forces you to look at your account and this is the first step in removing the fear associated with checking your account.

Secondly, it lets you know exactly where you are financially at this precise moment.

Visual Reinforcement

Visual reinforcement is a great way of keeping you motivated. Displaying your current progress will show you how you are gathering speed and momentum as time goes on.

That is what this next exercise is about.

Exercise 2

Take a large piece of paper and create a bar graph.

This is simply two columns.

On the left should be your total debt and on the right should be your total savings.

The simplest way of doing this would be to use 1cm for every £1000 which makes it easier to draw something that is to scale. (If you owe less than £10,000, then it may be better to use, 2 or even 3 cms per £1000 as this will allow you to visualize your progress better.)

Once you have done this, put the poster somewhere where you will see it daily. It's up to you how prominent this is in your house, but as long as you see it daily it will help keep you focused.

Using the figures above, your graph should look something like this:

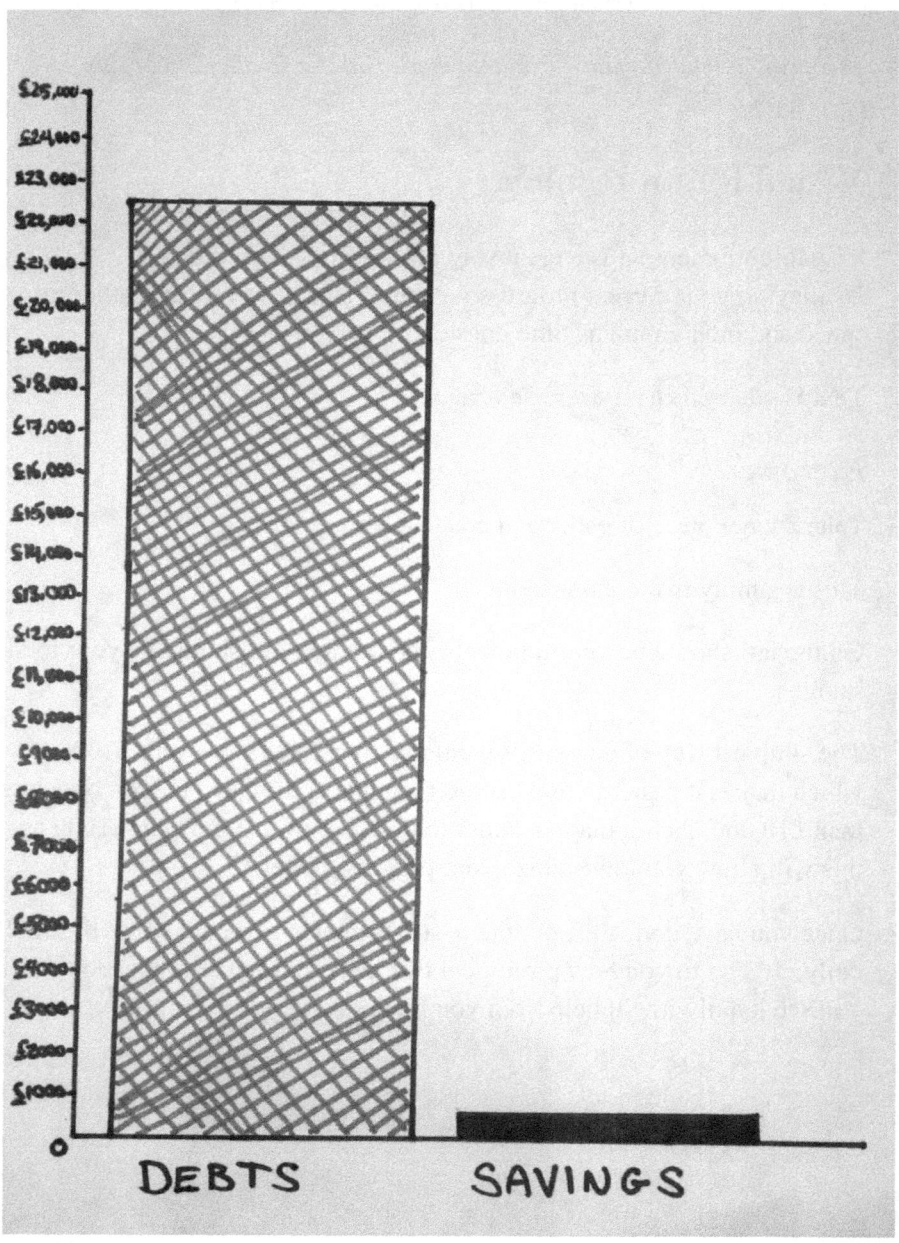

As you pay back debt and increase your savings, use a black pen to amend the appropriate part of the graph, by either filling in the red as it is paid off or by adding to the savings column. This will show you, in a very clear way, just how well you are doing.

Well done.

The journey can finally truly begin.

DAY 3. REVERSAL

Today your debt stops growing.

From this moment on, your debt will only decrease in size.

Today you stem the bleeding and from here on things can only improve. Your debt will shrink and freedom will take hold.

Today is a day for rejoicing in the reversal of the flow.

Reversing the flow

If you fire a rocket straight up into the atmosphere, there comes a point when the fuel runs out. At this point the rocket loses momentum and starts to return to Earth.

Now, there is a point, for a fraction of a second, when the rocket has stopped its ascent but has not yet begun its plummet back to earth.

This is where we are today.

The point where your debt stops growing and is about to start plummeting, gathering speed as it goes.

In order to make this happen, we need to ensure that the creditors do not have access to your credit card and that your credit card can no longer be used for day to day spending.

I remember a few years back I was given what was well-meaning, but potentially the worst advice I have ever received from a financial advisor. I was trying to reduce my debt and he told me to consolidate my credit card debts into one monthly payment and then freeze my credit card.

Literally.

I.e. he told me to put it in the freezer in a margarine tub full of water so that if I had to use it I would have to think about it first.

I did this and of course, as soon as the first emergency came along, I defrosted that card and used it.

It never went back in the freezer…

Right now we have to permanently put an end to debt's grip on your life.

It is drastic and it can feel traumatic but sometimes, in order to save your life, a traumatic operation is needed.

Exercise 1

Take a pair of scissors.

Cut your credit cards up.

Don't just cut them in half. Cut them into as many pieces as you can.

Destroy them.

Destroy them in the same way that they have destroyed your confidence, your peace of mind and your financial freedom.

These cards are not your friends.

If you have a partner, mark this day with a special (home cooked!) meal, maybe some candles and a glass of wine.

Make it a celebration.

The first victory in your battle against debt.

Hidden traps

This is the part where you will need to double check your last credit card statement.

This should no longer be scary as you already know how much you owe. You also know that your debt is not going to increase as a result of accidental credit card spending, so don't worry.

Go and get your credit card statement as we are now going to make sure that cutting up your cards has definitely put a stop to the cancer that is debt.

Exercise 2

Subscriptions.

It's time to check for subscription and hidden regular costs that may be coming off your credit card.

When I did this, I found that I was subscribing to Amazon Prime, even though I thought I had only signed up for a month's free trial.

I also found that my Netflix subscription was linked to my credit card, not my bank account as I had previously thought. These two things were creating more debt every month and I had no idea.

So, go through your statement and manually unlink or cancel every subscription that takes its payment from your credit card.

Some of the main culprits are iTunes, Amazon, Netflix, Hulu, Amazon Prime, Audible, etc.

You should also check for less common ones, for example, I once bought a digital weight loss and exercise product online only to later realise that I had accidentally also agreed to pay a monthly subscription to the author's website which, needless to say, I never used.

Once you have gone through and cancelled or unlinked your card from any of these subscriptions, make a note of how much you have stopped your debt from growing on a monthly basis. Remember that the reality is, that due to interest rates, your debt reduction is actually far greater than the simple cost of the subscriptions.

For example, if you cancel Amazon Prime (£4.99), Netflix (£5.99) and Audible (£7.99), you will have stopped your debt from growing, not by £227.64 per year (The total sum of your monthly subscriptions) but by £307.31 (based on a fairly standard 35% APR on credit cards).

Even if you keep those subscriptions and move them to direct debits, you will still have stopped your debt from growing by £80 that year.

That's money in your pocket, not in the bank's.

And another victory for you.

DAY 4. THE EMERGENCY FUND

So, you have cut up your credit cards.

Now what?

You may be asking yourself what you are going to do if any emergencies come up.

What if I need a plumber? Or my car breaks down?

What if a window breaks or I have sudden unexpected expenses? How am I going to pay for them now that my credit card is gone?

This is where the emergency fund comes in.

I heard someone once say, that there is only one thing we should always expect and that is the unexpected.

Life happens.

Things break.

Unplanned expenses will rear their heads.

It's time for you to be prepared for these occasions so that you control the situation, rather than the situation controlling you.

The emergency fund

You can call this what you like. Call it The Emergency Fund, the Rainy Day Fund, the OH CR*P, NOT AGAIN! Fund...

Call it whatever you want, as long as it is used solely and exclusively for emergencies.

This fund is not for holidays, new clothes, new cars, pizza or for when you have run out of milk. This is for those big emergencies that life is guaranteed to throw at you.

Now, I would suggest that, if you earn over £15,000 a year, you should aim for an emergency fund of £1,000 as this will cover the vast majority of unexpected emergencies.

If you earn less than that, aim for an emergency fund of £500.

You will be surprised at how quickly you can actually raise that money.

Put the funds into an account, that, whilst accessible, cannot be used on a daily basis.

Today we start building that emergency fund.

This is when we actually start pushing back against debt.

Exercise 1

Do you have any savings? Are your savings over £1000 already? If so, I am going to ask you to do something that may seem drastic. Take £1000 from your savings and put it into a separate account; your emergency fund.

If you currently don't have any savings, or your savings are not over £1000 then please skip this exercise and go to Exercise 2.

Congratulations, you have created an emergency fund and can now use Exercise 2 to start raising some funds to pay off some of your debts.

Positive Action

It's time to take positive action and start fighting back.

This is what this exercise is all about.

Exercise 2

Go through your house and find everything that you no longer use.

Books, DVDs, Video Games, musical instruments, furniture.

Anything.

Everything that you believe you could live without and that is still in working order.

Have you done that? Good.

Now start listing them on eBay, Gumtree, Craigslist and Facebook.

If the idea of internet sales sites is too daunting then take your items to a car boot sale/garage sale, but I would strongly recommend the eBay/Gumtree route.

If you are a first time eBay user and want to know how to list things, a quick search of YouTube turned up the following 15 minute video which may be of use to you: http://bit.ly/1umKwZ1.

As a quick aside, I would suggest that you list your items for ten days which means, if you list them on Thursday, that they will finish on Sunday evening. If you set the auction to end between 7.30 pm and 10pm, this is the sweet spot for eBay auctions as this is when many people will sit at home bidding on items.

Often, just taking positive action, even a small simple step like this, is enough to start the ball rolling and get the momentum going.

Good work.

DAY 5. MAKING YOUR MONEY COUNT

In case you were in any doubt, this system works on the simple premise of Stopping and reducing the Debt, Minimising Expenditure and Maximising Income.

Ultimately this is the real secret to getting out of debt. As you focus on maximising your income and minimising expenditure you will reduce debt very quickly and see very rapid results.

However, you must be willing to make sacrifices and take responsibility for the mistakes of your past. Making things right takes time and effort, but it will all be more than worthwhile in the end.

Today, we are going to take the first step towards maximising your income.

Today we start a BUDGET!

The Budget

What is a budget? Most people think a budget is a way of writing down on paper how much money is coming in and how much money needs to be spent on different items that month, or that week.

Whilst this is not a completely incorrect definition of what a budget is, I would like to expand on that and explain how a budget should work properly.

When you get together with your partner to plan the budget for the month, what you are actually doing is spending your money on paper. You are telling your money where to go rather than later wondering where it went.

Together you will spend your money on paper until there is no money left.

What this means is that you will both agree where your money is going. This means that later on, as the week or month goes by, (regardless of how much money is actually still in the bank) if something comes up that was not on the budget, you can, in all good conscience, truthfully say: "We don't have the money."

If you buy something that is not on budget, that has a massive knock on effect to the rest of the month as the money you have spent will have to come from something else. Often that tends to be a direct debit that gets returned, or a credit card payment that isn't made, leading on to a game of catch up and further financial problems.

Once you have created your budget, ***you must stick to it***.

Exercise 1 - Creating a Budget

I have put together a spreadsheet that will allow you to create a budget relatively quickly.

http://bit.ly/BgtPlSh

The aim of the budget is to make sure that your income and your spending are exactly the same. You must have no money left over at the end of the budget. This is known in the US as a "Zero-Dollar Budget", i.e. at the end of the budget there should be zero dollars left.

The reason for this is to ensure that your budget accounts for every penny as this way there is no doubt in relation to what you can buy and what is off the budget.

The budget sheet I have created has a box that changes colour to show you when your income and expenditure are equal. Use this to help you plan your spending.

When doing your budget, you must make sure that your basic necessities are covered first.

I would argue that you should first ensure that your house payment, be that mortgage or rent, is covered. This should then be followed by Food, Utilities (gas and electric), Transport, Clothing, Debt Repayment and then all other categories.

Your task now is to sit down (with your partner) and make a budget for the month.

Together.

You will argue. You may well find it boring.

You will get irritated and annoyed with each other but, once it's done and you have, together, told your money where to go, you will feel such a sense of relief that it will have all been worth it.

Make sure every penny is accounted for.

As you stick to it, you may find that it feels like you have had a pay rise as you won't be worrying about whether or not you have money to pay for the things you need.

Sticking to it

From today onwards you need to be accountable, either to yourself or, if you have a partner, to him or her.

In being accountable to each other you will be more disciplined but also have support when you need it. To make this easier, you need to make a note of everything you spend.

Exercise 2

Every time you buy a coffee, or do the groceries shopping, or pay for parking or buy a train ticket or fill up your car with fuel, make a note of it.

This can be in a notebook or on your phone or on anything else that won't get lost or destroyed!

The aim of this is not to keep track of what is in your account (although this is an added bonus) but rather to give you an awareness of what you are spending your money on.

This will allow for better budgeting but will also make you think twice about buying things.

You won't have to do this for ever, but for now, until you get to a point where you no longer need to do this, I would like you to continue to note down your spending.

At the end of each day, get together with your partner and review your spending as this will force you to talk about it, ensuring that what could become a taboo subject for you as a couple is brought out into the open.

Today is all about taking back control of your money.

You are in charge.

    You are the boss.

DAY 6. NEW SPENDING HABITS

Now we put the budget to the test.

It is important to remember that you won't get your budget right first time.

You may find that you have over budgeted for food and under budgeted for fuel or vice versa.

The important thing to remember is that any changes to your spending that take place need to be discussed before they happen.

Today you are going to test your budget setting skills!

These two exercises will help you in both sticking to your budget and in tweaking your budget to make it as realistic as possible.

Groceries

This is usually the biggest expenditure for a family outside of mortgage/rent payments (although not necessarily for singles or a couple where fuel and transport costs could be more expensive).

This is why it is so important to make sure that the weekly groceries shop doesn't get out of hand.

This is what we will tackle today.

Exercise 1

Sit down (with your partner) and plan your meals for the next seven days.

Every meal.

Every snack.

(If you were looking at starting a diet, this would be a great time to start!)

As you plan your meals, work out what ingredients you will need, check to see what you have got and write a shopping list together.

Check what other items you may need, e.g. toiletries and cleaning products, etc and write these down too.

I would suggest you type this up and print it out if this is a viable option, if not then write your shopping list in one column down one side of the page. The reason for this will become apparent in Exercise 2.

The Weekly Shop

There are two tricks to completing the weekly shop whilst on a budget that I find very helpful:

1. Make a list *and stick to it!* Only buy items that are written down. If they are not written down then you cannot buy them. Obviously, if you have forgotten one or two small items, that is not a problem, but you should write them down on your list as you buy them. This will keep you from buying things that you do not need or things *"That just looked so good!"* or that *"were such a bargain!"* If they are not on your list, they are not essential and are therefore a waste of money.

2. Don't go shopping on an empty stomach. This makes you prone to buying snacks that you otherwise would not have bought. This all adds to your bill.

Exercise 2

Go shopping.

As you go around the shop, write down how much each item costs so that later you can use these figures to help you budget better.

You may eventually get to a point where, not including any special offers, you know exactly how much your weekly food bill will come to before you even get to the shop.

As you go around the store, keep a running total going so that you know you are not going to go over your budget.

This is not something that you will need to do every time, but until you can stick to your list without thinking, you should do this.

When I first did this I found a great freedom in knowing that I no longer had to worry about whether or not my shopping was going to come to more than I had planned.

I no longer had to worry about whether I had enough money to pay for the shopping.

    I was finally in control and you can be too.

DAY 7. FAMILY

Most people start plans like this on a Monday.

Therefore, by my maths, today should be Sunday.

There is no arduous task today.

No writing.

No planning.

No calculations or goal setting.

Today I just want you to spend time with your family and friends.

Go for a walk.

Go to a park.

Go for a bicycle ride.

Do something together.

My only stipulation is that it should not cost you anything.

Drive to the beach and take a picnic.

Make some popcorn and watch a movie.

Do whatever makes you and your family happy.

No budget related exercises today, just time to enjoy with the people who are most precious to you.

And remember this: The best things in life really are free.

Enjoy your weekend.

DAY 8. SNOWBALL

The Snowball is all about making a start on aggressively reducing your debt.

I am going to suggest something that is not very popular with many financial gurus/financial advisors.

If you look back to Day 2, I asked you to list your debt in order of size. I did not mention interest rates.

This is the order in which I want you to start repaying them. I don't want you to worry about the interest rates for each debt. In fact, don't even look at them.

A lot of people will call this crazy, short sighted or just plain stupid, but I don't care.

The reality is that neither you or I were particularly financially savvy when we got into debt. If we had been, we would not have ended up at the point where our debt was this bad and we would almost definitely not be reading this book or following this plan!

So, trust me on this.

The Snowball part of this plan is about creating small victories that spur you on, keep you motivated and as you win each small battle, the war becomes easier to fight and therefore easier to win.

Where to start

The first place to start is by looking again at your savings.

If you do not have your emergency fund in place, because you simply did not have the savings required to do so in the first place, then feel free to skip this exercise and move on to Exercise 2.

If you already had more than £1000 savings in the bank, then continue reading.

Exercise 1

Use your savings to pay down your debts.

There is no point having savings that accumulate 3% to 5% per year when your debts are attracting anything from 6% to 35% interest per year.

Let me give you an example:

John Smith has £1000 credit card debt at 19% APR. (Annual Percentage Rate)

He also has £1000 in savings (not his emergency fund). This is not in an investment account, it is just in a standard savings fund. He is quite fortunate in that he was able to get a higher rate of 5% APR on his savings.

At the end of the year his savings will have grown to a "massive" £1050.

His debt will have increased to £1190.

He will owe £140 more than his savings grew.

Or, he could take those savings and pay off his debt therefore saving himself £140 that year.

That saving can then be used to either pay off more debt, save or add to his budget.

So, Exercise 1 is *use any surplus savings (above your £1000 emergency fund) and start paying off your debts.*

Smallest debt first.

You will feel so much better when you realise that instead of five debts, you now only have four. Or three.

Or even two.

The other debts will soon be gone too.

Gathering speed

This exercise is all about learning how the Snowball method works and starting to pay back your debts.

You will quickly see that, as you stick with this method, the number of debts you have will decrease and the amount you are able to pay back on each debt will quickly increase.

Exercise 2

Take the list of debts you wrote on Day 2 and next to each debt write down the minimum payment.

The aim of the snowball is that as you pay off one debt, you then use that minimum payment to add to the payment of the next debt and so on.

For example:

Jane Smith has four debts as follows:

Credit Card A - £2000 (Minimum Payment of £42)

Credit Card B - £3400 (Minimum Payment of £64)

Car Loan - £5500 (Minimum Payment of £210)

Home Improvement Loan - £7500 (Minimum Payment of £320)

Please note that these are arbitrary figures and are for illustration purposes only.

Jane takes some savings, works some overtime and finds she is able to pay off Credit Card A in the first month.

The following month she pays Credit Card B's minimum payment, plus the minimum payment from Credit Card A, so ends up paying £106 per month.

She works really hard and pays that off over the next few months and then starts work on her Car Loan and now the minimum amount she will pay off is £316 per month (That loan's minimum payment plus the minimum payment from the other two loans.)

As you can see, the debt repayment can quickly gather speed and momentum and the results will come much quicker than you expect.

So, write down your minimum payments and work out how you are going to pay off your smallest debt in the shortest amount of time.

Having done this, I would suggest that you take however much you can afford right now and pay a little extra off your smallest debt. Even if it's just £5 or £10 you will have made a start and will have taken your first step towards reducing your debt.

Let's get this Snowball rolling!

DAY 9. MINIMISE EXPENDITURE

As you know, this plan works on the principles of Stopping Debt, Minimising Expenditure and Maximising Income.

Today we are going to look at another way of minimising our monthly expenditure.

Insurance

This is an area in which people often get a bit lazy. I was the same.

Every year my insurance renewal quote comes through and the letter tells me not to do anything and it will automatically renew. It's normally slightly lower than the year before so I just let it self-renew and don't think anything more of it.

Or at least that's what I used to do.

Eighteen months ago or so I decided to check to see how competitive my insurance renewal quote really was.

I headed over to the comparison websites and it took me approximately 30 minutes to save myself £416. My insurance dropped from £840 to £424. That's a massive saving.

I texted my wife and told her that for the last 30 minutes I had made money like a millionaire! I mean, if I were to work a 40 hour week earning £836 an hour, I would earn £1,738,880 a year. I'm pretty certain that puts me squarely in the millionaire bracket!

I then went and did the same with our home insurance, life insurance and pet insurance. (In fact, I cancelled the pet insurance as I had been paying into it for years and had only made one claim so decided to rely on my emergency fund instead, which saved me a further £16 a month...)

Exercise 1

Go to online comparison websites and get new quotes for your insurance policies. Don't worry about any policies that are provided for you by your work, but make sure that you are not duplicating these policies with your own.

Do them in the following order, as this is the order that will get you the quickest and most significant results:

1. Car Insurance.
2. House Insurance.
3. Life Insurance.
4. Others.

It is worth remembering that often people have a separate mobile phone (cell phone) insurance policy when in reality it is likely to be covered by your home insurance if it is damaged at home, and very often bank accounts offer phone insurance as part and parcel of their current account.

Make sure you are not insured twice on the same item as you can only claim on one of the policies!

Also, when you have your new insurance quotes, make sure you find out how much your current insurer is going to charge for cancelling early as this may not make the saving worth it. It's probably not worth changing insurance provider if your £65 a year saving is going to be eaten up by the £60 administration fee that your current provider may charge.

What next?

Again, like yesterday, you need to make positive steps away from the mentality of spending the extra money you may feel you now have.

Exercise 2

Work out how much money you have saved every month as a result of changing your insurance policies and set up a standing order to that value from your current account into your emergency fund.

If your emergency fund is already at £1000 then use the excess to pay off your debts, smallest to largest.

Your standard of living will not decline as a result of paying more off your debts as you were already paying that money to your insurance company anyway. Instead you have found a way to pay down your debts much quicker!

DAY 10. FUTURE PLANNING

Today is all about future proofing our finances.

How often have you been in a situation where you suddenly find that you have to pay a large amount of money on something completely unexpected?

Like Christmas. (No one told me it was on the 25th December this year!)

Or the car tax.

Or school fees.

Or a utility bill. (Some people still pay these quarterly…)

These are bills that we know are coming. We know we are going to have to pay them and we know how much they are going to be, yet we always seem to end up scrabbling and scrimping for money on the month when these bills come in.

The reality is that this is not due to the bills being overly expensive or us not being able to afford them, it simply comes down to poor planning.

Most large companies have what is known as a Sink Fund. A Sink Fund is a fund that is topped up regularly in anticipation of a large future expense, for example; when a company buys a property they assess many things, including the roof. If the roof will have to be replaced in twenty years time, they estimate the cost of replacing the roof and incorporate it into their business plan, putting aside a certain amount of money every year in order to cover that cost. If replacing the roof is going to cost £20,000 then they put £1000 aside every year in order to do this. That equates to approximately £84 a month, which, as a business, is more than manageable, whereas finding £20,000 in one go could be an enormous challenge.

We need to do the same with our bills in order to future proof our finances. Not only will this mean that you can afford to pay your bills when they come in, but you'll also find that, by having the money ready, your stress and worry levels will be greatly reduced.

Planning

In order to know how much to put aside, it is important to know what will be required.

You need to take everything into consideration.

How many new tyres will your car need this year?

How much will it cost to service the car?

How much would you like to spend on Christmas this year?

What other large bills will be coming in?

Exercise 1

Sit down (with your partner) and work out what bills you will have in the next 12 months.

Also write down how much they are and when they are due.

Write this down in your journal/notebook like this:

Bill	Amount	Due
Christmas	*£150*	*1st December*
Car Service/MOT	*£250*	*27th August*
Car Tax	*£140*	*30th March*

And so on.

Now work out the total amount you have to pay every year. (Which in this example would be £540.)

Then divide that number by 12 and there is the monthly amount you need to put aside, in this case £45.

Take Action

It's now time to do something about this. By now you already know my thoughts on taking positive steps as soon as possible!

Exercise 2

Firstly create an online savings account (this is usually very easy to do if you have internet banking).

Then set up a standing order for the monthly amount that you arrived at in Exercise 1 so that over the next few months this will start to build up. Then when the time comes, use that money to cover the large bills that are now planned for.

DAY 11. CARS

It's time now to look at car finance.

This is often the biggest expenditure that people have after their rent/mortgage, but it really shouldn't be.

Cars are the worst investment any one can make (unless you specialise in classic cars, but I'm going to assume that this is not the case…)

As soon as you drive your car off the forecourt it drops in value by literally thousands of pounds/dollars.

If you buy a brand new car you will lose *at least* a third of its value the moment it leaves that forecourt.

Would you like to know a secret?

Rich people don't buy brand new cars.

Rich people tend to buy cars that are a couple of years old. And they don't buy them on finance.

"But I need a car!" I hear you say. And I'll be honest; I totally agree. Nowadays it is almost impossible to get by without a car.

There are always exceptions to this rule, however, most modern families need a car. I'm not disputing this.

What I do want to question is whether you actually need *the car you currently own*.

When we get right down to it, cars serve one only purpose; to get you and your passengers from A to B.

Of course it's nice to have a car which looks nice and fills you with pleasure as you drive.

Of course it's nice to have the latest satnav and reclining seats, and a DVD player and the latest Bluetooth enabled audio system.

But that's all it is: just nice.

It's *not* essential.

So, I want you to look out the window at the car you are driving and I want you to answer two questions:

1. Does your car payment cost more than a quarter of what is left of your take-home income after having paid your mortgage?

2. Is your car worth more than a quarter of your annual take home salary?

If you answered yes to either of these questions then its time you changed your car…

Exercise 1

If you answered yes to the questions I just asked, then it is time to take action.

Your first task today is to find out how much you could sell your current car for.

Be realistic and do your research. If your car is not in great condition, then aim for a slightly lower valuation and be prepared to be pleasantly surprised.

When it comes to it, don't undervalue your car as you need to get the highest price you can in order to make the biggest dent in your debt.

Exercise 2

Now do some research to find out how much you really need in order to get a car that will do the job you need, i.e. getting you and your family from A to B.

For example, a single person is unlikely to need a 7-seater, an estate or even a saloon car and may well be able to get around quite happily in a small 2 door, 4-seater vehicle. (I'm thinking Nissan Micra and Ford Ka type cars, although I am not specifically promoting them!)

A family with four children will probably need a 7-seater, but they don't need the latest model.

All you need in a car is function and a modicum of reliability.

Exercise 3

Now I want you to look at selling your current, expensive car in order to buy a cheaper car.

Use the difference in value between the two to either complete your emergency fund or pay off a large chunk of your debt (or both!)

Remember, this is not a long-term thing.

You will be able to get a nice car again, just not while you're trying to pay off your debt.

This may mean a couple of years of sacrifice, a couple of years driving a wreck, but at the end of it, it will have been worth it.

It's time to take the money that you have tied up in a hunk of metal outside your house and put it to good use breaking off some of the chains of debt that are currently holding you back.

I realise that you may not be able to sell the car today, but I want you to take positive steps towards that goal so that within the next few days, if necessary, your car will be on the market with a view to selling it very soon.

If your car is a lease car or is on a hire/purchase scheme, contact the company from which you got the car and see if they will take it back with no extra charges.

Explain that you can no longer afford to keep paying the monthly payments and normally they will take the car back as it is in their interest to have the car returned to them rather than have you default on your payments.

This will free up a good amount of cash to enable you to buy a small run around to keep you going and then make bigger overpayments on your debts.

The only exception to this rule is if your car is a company car and your company is paying for you to have it as this should not affect your salary apart from in terms of having to pay slightly higher taxes. If this is the case then the benefits of having the car paid for by the company will vastly outweigh the added expense of slightly higher taxes.

DAY 12. GET THE FAMILY INVOLVED

As you can probably see by now, becoming debt free is something that will affect your whole family.

In order to make it more sustainable in the long run, it is a great idea to get the family involved.

I remember how excited the children were when I asked them what ideas they had to help us save money.

Now, it's not always easy to explain to them why we need to save money, but, for my children at least, when I told them that we needed to try to save up for a bigger house and that therefore we had to start spending less, they were enthused and full of ideas.

This also made it easier later on when I had to tell them that they could not have something if it wasn't in the budget. Don't get me wrong, they were often still upset, but at least they understood that there was a reason when I had to tell them "no."

Family Time

Exercise 1

When you have some time this evening, maybe over dinner, explain to your children that you are trying to save money and that you need their help.

Encourage them to come up with ways they can help save or make money and then help them make these ideas a reality.

Here are some ideas to help you get started:

- Get them to make a poster illustrating your progress towards your emergency fund then get them to put it up somewhere.
- Ask them if there are any toys they have that they no longer play with that they are willing to sell. Tell them they'll get to keep some of the money!
- Ask them to come up with their own ideas for ways of saving money, e.g. walking or cycling instead of driving, turning off lights to save electricity, giving up expensive snacks or eating out, etc.

Doing this as a family will help draw your whole family into the journey and will make it a joint victory, along with teaching them valuable life lessons along the way.

DAY 13. REVIEW DAY

I'd like you to get into the habit of regularly reviewing your finances.

Keeping on top of your finances and being aware of how much you have coming in and going out makes you more conscious of your money habits and helps you get away from that feeling of dread when it comes to checking your accounts.

It also stops you from overspending and ending up in a position where direct debits start being returned (along with the hefty charges this incurs.)

Budget Review

So, this first exercise is about making sure that you are sticking to your budget.

There is no point making a budget if you (and your family) are not sticking to it as this just makes it a pointless, demotivating and ultimately soul destroying task.

So, if you have gone over budget this week, don't despair, simply work out whether this was unavoidable (in which case adjust your budget accordingly) or whether this was through bad habits creeping back in.

If it was as a result of bad habits then you are now in a position to identify what triggered that behaviour and put steps in place to prevent it from happening again.

Exercise 1

Check your bank account. If possible, print off a full statement and check it against the notes you have made about your spending, i.e. your spending diary. This way you'll be able to spot any discrepancies or any extra transactions that you did not write down.

Then check that you are still on track with your budget for the month and make any necessary adjustments as you see fit.

Just remember that you cannot create money from nothing. Any adjustments you make to one area of the budget must be reflected in another.

A Challenge

As I explained earlier, food shopping is usually the biggest expenditure that modern families make on a regular basis, so whatever we can do to reduce this cost will help.

Exercise 2

Like last week, plan your meals.

Yep, all of them.

Then write your shopping list.

This time though, I want you to try and see if you can buy all the items on your list for less than you spent last week.

This may involve going to a different supermarket (In the UK, Lidl and Aldi have surprisingly high quality food for a much lower price than mainstream supermarkets.)

Or it could involve replacing branded goods for Supermarket own goods, economy value goods or even using coupons and discount vouchers.

Set yourself a challenge and start to enjoy the satisfaction there is to be found in making savings.

Every penny you save is another step closer to being debt free.

The challenge is set!

DAY 14. A DAY FOR FAMILY & FRIENDS

Well done! You have completed another week in your journey towards being debt free.

Again, I want you to have the day off. You don't need to worry about your money today because you have put things in motion to revert the cycle and, even though it may not necessarily feel like it, you are already well on your way towards clearing your debt.

So, relax.

Enjoy your day with your family and friends doing all those inexpensive things that you love doing together.

And if you're worried about your children not having expensive things that other kids have, I can guarantee that when they are older they won't remember the expensive toys or costly meals out.

They will remember you and the time you spent with them.

They'll remember the movies you watched together.

They'll remember playing hide and seek in the park.

They'll remember the bike rides.

The time spent colouring in together.

The time spent reading stories together.

So go and build some memories that will outlast anything that money could ever buy.

DAY 15. EBAY

If you listed your items for a ten day auction then they should have finished last night.

This means that many people will have already paid for you to send them the items.

Now we can start using this extra income to take us closer towards our goal of becoming debt free.

It is vitally important that this sudden influx of extra cash is not seen as an opportunity to go out and buy things.

That is not why you listed your items on eBay. The money you have made is already earmarked to either add to your emergency fund (up to £1000) or to start paying off debts.

It is not there for pizza, clothes or the latest electronic gadgets!

Using the money wisely

So, you have now successfully sold your items on eBay and the items have been paid for.

This leads us nicely to today's exercises.

Exercise 1

Package and post the items you have sold so that you know exactly how much you have left after fees and postage costs have been covered (i.e. your net profit.)

Exercise 2

Deposit the money into your account. Be aware that if you used PayPal there may be some fees, which will be deducted from you when you transfer it.

Once the money has arrived in your account use all of it *immediately* to increase your emergency fund towards the £1000 target or, if you already have a £1000 emergency fund, to pay off some of your debt.

Always follow the plan though. Use all of the money towards your smallest debt, until the smallest debt is gone.

Then, if there is still something left after paying off your smallest debt, start on the next smallest debt.

Every time you pay off some debt or add to your emergency fund, adjust your bar graph accordingly (see Day 2) as this will allow you to visibly track your success.

You are awesome and have already accomplished so much in these last two weeks.

Keep up the good work like this and you will very soon be debt free!

DAY 16. MAXIMISE INCOME

In order to aggressively start paying back your debt it is important to not only minimise your expenditure but also to maximise your income.

For some people this may appear to be a very difficult task, but here is the reality:

Even those of us who work 40 hours per week (a relatively standard number of hours for most people in the UK) and assuming that we all sleep 8 hours per night, we are only using 35% of our waking time at work.

This leaves 65% of our waking time in which we could be increasing our income.

Now, don't get me wrong, I'm not saying that you should be working every waking moment, I'm just pointing out that we have far more time than often we realise.

I am a strong believer that time with your family and friends is highly important and should not be sacrificed purely to make money.

You should also make time for your other interests, hobbies and activities as these, along with your family, are what make your life interesting and give you purpose, satisfaction and quality of life.

However, having said that, you would be amazed at how much extra you could earn by simply working one or two evenings a week.

Taking on a pizza delivery job two evenings a week, or working as a cashier at a local supermarket a couple of evenings or afternoons a week will boost your monthly income by a good amount. You could earn anywhere from £200 to £600 extra a month (depending on how many extra hours you are willing and able to work.)

The other option for increasing your income would be to look into whether your current occupation allows you the option of working overtime.

I know how easy it is to turn down overtime, but this really is one of the simplest ways to earn extra income as it doesn't involve learning any new skills, has less of an effect on your taxes (at least here in the UK) and is also a familiar environment.

The negative side of relying on overtime is that it cannot be guaranteed every month.

Imagine being able to pay an extra £300 or £400 a month off your debt every month. It could make the difference between paying off your debt in four years to paying off your debt in two years.

Once you're debt free you'll have the choice to either continue working these jobs and using the extra income to build wealth, or to simply spend more time with your family, being able to make use of the extra available income from having no debt repayments.

I personally could not imagine anything more fulfilling.

Making a start

Today's task is all about taking positive steps towards finding a means of increasing your income.

Don't worry if you are unable to start increasing your income today, as long as you are taking the right steps towards doing this.

Exercise 1

Speak to your manager or supervisor and explain that you are interested in any overtime that may be available in the near future. You don't need to disclose why you want to work extra, simply that you are willing to do it.

Ask them to call you first for any emergency overtime that may come up or even if any future overtime needs to be planned.

You'll probably find that if you tell them this and accept overtime when they offer it, you will start getting more and more offers of work. Supervisors, like most of us, will always take the easy route when completing a task. If their task is to find someone to take on some overtime and they know that you are reliable and will usually accept it, they will phone you first rather than risk wasting time on calls to people who may turn them down.

Exercise 2

If overtime is not an option, or you would rather do something different, then your task today is to look at the jobs section of your local paper/employment website and start looking for an evening job.

Often the easiest jobs to get are in places that have high staff turn over and that allow for evening work.

Examples of these would include:

- Pizza Delivery Driver
- Cashiers/Til operators
- Shopping Delivery Drivers
- Warehouse work.
- Factory work.

Just remember, when you are looking at these jobs: You are not looking for a career in these industries.

This is a means to an end. It is for a finite period of time and therefore, while the job may not be something that you would choose to do, it is a means of bringing some extra income into your household so that you can pay off your debt earlier and experience the freedom that comes from living debt free!

DAY 17. TRAVEL

Almost every single one of us has to travel to get to work.

Nowadays it's quite rare for people to live close enough to walk to work, so commuting is a large part of our every day expenses.

Today I'd like to look at ways in which we can reduce the cost of our commute and therefore minimise our expenditure in this area.

Some ideas

Here's the reality of the situation: we enjoy our time in the car. (At least I do!)

There is something peaceful about being able to get in the car on your own, select the music, radio station or audiobook that you want and set off on your journey to work. No disruption and no interruptions.

No children calling your name.

No tasks to do.

Some quality "me-time".

But here's the thing: In every car in the queue of traffic is another person, sat alone, slowly fighting their way through the congestion, burning money in the form of fuel.

It may be time to sacrifice your current "me-time" in order to focus on your future.

I used to drive to work. I only lived two miles from the office, but I would get up every morning and drive those two miles. On a good day it took me less than 6 minutes to get there.

I must admit; I didn't have the most economical of cars, but it wasn't awful either, however, I worked out that it was costing me about £240 a year in fuel, just to get to and from work. That was not including all the other short trips I took, like driving round the corner to the shop because I was a little too lazy to walk.

And that's just it; we could save so much money by cutting down on our car use.

For example, if someone lives 5 miles from their work place, chances are that there are good bus links to get them there.

Some quick research online shows that an annual bus pass in a large city such as Cardiff or Birmingham, costs around £1 ($0.70) per day with unlimited travel. Assuming your journey to and from work is a 10 mile round trip, in the UK this would cost you approximately £600 ($940) a year in fuel, not including the cost of wear and tear on your vehicle and tyres, which could easily add on another £100 - £200 ($150 - $300) a year.

By getting a bus pass you could save yourself up to £435 ($680) a year.

That's a holiday.

That's Christmas paid for.

That's almost half of that £1000 ($1500) you owe on that credit card!

Exercise 1

In this exercise I want you to consider the practicalities of the following modes of transport.

The aim is to work out which one of these would be both practical but also more economical in the long run.

Please write down the pros and cons for each method of getting to work along with the appropriate costs involved.

1. Bus Pass

2. Car Pool/Lift Sharing

3. Cycling

4. Walking/Jogging

5. Driving alone

Exercise 2

If you have completed Exercise 1 objectively then the challenge of this exercise is to now take some time to work our how you are going to start traveling to work using the best, most efficient and effective form of transport.

If for you this is lift sharing, then contact your local co-workers and see if any of them are interested.

If it is cycling then dust off that rusty mountain bike, put some oil on the chain, wipe the cobwebs from your bike helmet and get yourself ready for the ride to work.

Before you know it your journey to work, whilst different, will be just as enjoyable as it was before.

DAY 18. CAREER DREAMS AND ASPIRATIONS

According to data released by Gallup in 2013, only 13% of people are actually engaged in their jobs. In other words, 87% of people are not emotionally involved with their work.

People, in general are not happy at work.

That's massive.

That needs to change.

Are you in that 87%. Do you find your work boring, unsatisfying or simply not engaging?

I know you are capable of so much more than you are currently achieving so I want you to believe and dream with me.

There are two reasons people work:

1. To earn money.
2. Because they love what they do and are passionate about the results they get or the people they work with.

My suggestion to you is that if you are not achieving both these things in your current employment then you should look at getting a different job.

I must stress one thing though:

<u>DO NOT QUIT YOUR JOB UNTIL YOU HAVE ANOTHER ONE LINED UP!</u>

This is one of the biggest mistakes people make. They leave their current employment simply because they don't like their job.

This would set you back and would turn everything you have been working towards upside down and you would quickly end up in much worse debt than you have ever been in before.

You would be giving up on your income, the main source from which you are paying down your debt. This is the exact opposite of what we are trying to achieve.

Dreaming Big

It's time to dream big.

In order to find that dream job, you first need to know what it is exactly that you are looking for.

You may think that you want to be a children's book author or a full time musician, a teacher, a business owner or any number of other things, and I honestly believe your dreams are within your reach.

You may not get there today or tomorrow, but if you persevere then in the end I know you can get there.

I want you to have as much fun as possible, whilst earning as much as you can on the way and this is what today's exercises are about.

Exercise 1

Write down what you ideal career/job would be.

Now write down the five things that most attract you to that career.

For example:

Full time Musician

1. Being able to make music every day.//
2. Being recognised for my creativity.
3. Making money.
4. Fame.
5. Getting sponsored by big name guitar companies.

Reality

Now, the reality is that landing your dream job may not be an easy thing to do, however, what we have done in the last exercise is clarify what it is we really want to do and achieve every day.

Using the above example, there are many roles out there that will allow you to make music every day (assuming that you are able to do so, of course!)

You could become a music teacher, or play in old people's homes, teaching the elderly or teaching people with special needs.

You could provide musical services to people on sites like fiverr.com where people pay different amounts of money for you to write them a jingle, or to write and record a song for them.

My point is this: You do not have to give up on your dream in order to earn money, but rather, you should aim to find a job or a career that incorporates those things that most attract you to your dream job.

This way you will not only be doing something that brings you immense satisfaction but you'll also be earning money as you do it.

Exercise 2

Look at your list of dream job qualities and now list as many other jobs you can think of that would allow you to achieve and experience these things.

Really think hard about this.

What is it about those things that you find so attractive?

Why is that?

This might reveal unexpected things about yourself and you might find yourself writing down careers and jobs that you may not have previously expected to be interested in.

Once you have these jobs written down, start looking in classified sections and job boards and online and start applying for interviews.

This is about living a fulfilling and satisfying life, so do not take a job that offers large amounts of money but no job satisfaction or enjoyment. Equally, do not take a job that offers all the satisfaction you need but no money.

It's time to start living the life you always dreamed you would.

As an aside, if you are one of the fortunate few in a job that you love and that pays enough then congratulations! Continue doing everything you can to be the best at what you do and you will soon be reaping even more rewards than you have been so far!

DAY 19. ALL ABOUT YOU

Ultimately this book is about making your life better.

It's about improving the quality of your life.

It is very hard to stick to things if there is no enjoyment along the way.

I know that breaking through the struggles is something that is to be celebrated, however, even soldiers need time out during a war, otherwise surrender becomes much more likely.

This is what today is about.

Today I want us to work out how we can win this war on debt whilst still having fun, leaving us with something to show for it at the end.

Entertainment

Saying "No" to all forms of entertainment in the interest of clearing debt will quickly result in burn out.

What many people don't realise is just how easy (and often more fun) it is to create your own entertainment.

For example, if you love watching movies with your children, rather than paying £50 for a trip to the cinema (with the added expense of cinema popcorn), why not use a Saturday afternoon transforming your living room into a cinema?

You could rent a movie from any number of online retailers (Amazon, iTunes, Netflix, Hulu, etc) and have "movie" popcorn from a local shop all for less than £5.

If your children want to make the experience even more realistic they can do what mine do and make their own cinema tickets which they collect as people come in.

Alternatively, if you prefer to be outdoors, why not go for a cycle ride, a run or a walk.

If you like eating out, why not find a recipe online for your favourite take out or restaurant food and cook it at home for a fraction of the price and probably much more flavour?

Everything is possible.

Exercise 1

With your family, write down all your favourite forms of entertainment, including why you enjoy that particular activity.

Now write down as many ideas as possible in relation to how you would do these things for a fraction of the price.

From now on, put these ideas into practice and have fun!

Savings

I know that I earlier said that having large amounts of savings whilst still in debt is not a sensible thing to do but I do believe it is never too early to start cultivating a habit of saving money.

What this will do is protect you from falling back into your old ways once you have cleared your debt as you will have created the new habit of *saving* to replace the habit of *spending*.

It also allows you to actually have something to show for your hard work.

Exercise 2

Create an online savings account and set up a standing order for £10 per month to go into that account.

That account is for holidays, or long term savings, or Christmas or whatever you want it to be for. It is yours to use as you will. My only suggestion is that you don't use it to pay off debt, unless you get to a point where your savings could pay off the last of your debt and you desperately want to clear that last little bit.

Once you clear your debt, I would suggest that you put at least 10% of your income into that account, if not more, as this will keep you from overspending whilst also giving you something for the future.

After all, securing a debt free future is the main reason you are doing this.

DAY 20. WEEKLY REVIEW

As you know by now, today is the day for your weekly review. You should find that you are getting better at sticking to your budget.

If you are finding sticking to the budget difficult then I'd like you to try the envelope system.

Envelope System

If you have not heard of the envelope system, this is possibly the oldest method of successful budgeting. Its the one your grandmother probably used.

This method, if used correctly, makes it impossible to overspend and this is what today's exercises are about.

Exercise 1

Plan your weekly shopping trip as you have been doing the last few weeks.

Use a shopping list as you have been.

Now move on to Exercise 2.

Exercise 2

Having worked out your weekly shopping budget, withdraw that amount in cash and place it in an envelope marked "Groceries".

Do the same for "Fuel" and any other regular cash spending. Personally I only did this for Groceries and Fuel, but you may have other things you need to spend cash on.

Once you have put the cash in the appropriate envelopes, take your cards out of your wallet and put them away somewhere safe.

The cards are no longer an option so you have to stick to using cash.

When the cash in the envelope runs out you cannot buy anything else until the following week.

It is that simple and it definitely works.

It will force you to start thinking about every item you buy.

You will add up as you go along and you will learn not to overspend.

If you use this in conjunction with your spending diary you will feel like you have had a pay rise as, when you think hard about how to spend your money, you'll find it stretches much further than you thought it could!

Use this method for as long as you need.

Some people find they can stick to a budget without using envelopes but personally I found this method to be a lifesaver.

Use whatever you need to help you stick to your budget and before you know it you won't ever worry about how much you can spend as sticking to your budget it will become second nature.

DAY 21. THE END

Congratulations!

You are a true revolutionary.

You have kicked back against Society's culture of debt and have decided to take matters into your own hand.

You are now equipped with all the tools you need to finish your war on debt and I know that you can and will succeed.

Remember; there is no such thing as a small victory. Every victory deserves to be celebrated.

So, take time today to relax with your family.

Maybe you could get a bottle of wine to share with your partner.

Or a take-away.

Just make sure it is within your budget. I do not want you falling back into your old habits…

Enjoy your day today and make sure you read the next chapter as this will explain how to maintain the momentum and keep you on the road towards a completely debt free lifestyle.

For today, however, just relax and enjoy the feeling of having come so far and achieved so much in such a short space of time.

Maybe look back at all the battles you have won over the last three weeks and remember how it felt to be beating your debt down.

You are a winner.

    You are a true revolutionary.

DAY 22. THE FUTURE BEGINS

Amazing.

You have spent the last 21 days turning your life around.

If you have followed the program as it's set out you will have made massive inroads into paying off your debt.

New spending and saving habits will be forming and now your debt is finally retreating.

You are in control.

You now tell your money where it should go rather than wondering where it went.

You are aggressively tackling the debt that has built up in your life and whether it is £500 or £50,000, that debt will soon be history because you have decided to make it so.

What Next?

As you have probably worked out, whilst this battle is won, the war is not yet over.

You have dealt the enemy a lethal blow. You have cut off its source so your debt can no longer grow, but there is still some work to do before this war can truly be won.

In order to defeat debt once and for all, a long-term strategy needs to be put in place.

To do this we must identify short-term targets in order to reach your long-term goal.

It is time for one final exercise.

Exercise 1

I'm certain you have heard of SMART goals before.

These are goals that are:

Specific

Measurable

Actionable

Realistic

Time-Specific

As the saying goes; "How do you eat an elephant?" "One mouthful at a time."

Each goal will bring you closer to your ultimate debt free destination.

I would like you to write down 5 goals that you want to achieve in the next 2 months.

They can be anything you like as long as they are SMART, e.g:

Goal 1:

Complete my emergency fund (Specific).

I need £600 to do this. (Measurable)

I will do this by working 20 hours overtime per month. (Actionable)

My boss has told me that there is at least 20 hours overtime available to me this month if I want it. (Realistic)

I will do this within four weeks. (Time-Specific)

Write out 5 goals to complete within the next two months, focusing on Reducing Debt, Minimising Expenditure and Maximising Income.

As you focus on smaller, achievable goals you will be consistently winning.

Don't be disheartened if you miss some of your deadlines, or don't quite complete your goal in the time limit you set, just renew your resolve and remember that every small step you take is another step towards a debt-free life.

Victory

As you gather momentum you will quickly find that this first 21 day battle, arguably the hardest of them all, will fade from your memory and will become a story you tell your children.

You will tell the tale of this turning point.

Of the battle that swung the war in your favour.

Of the struggle that damaged the enemy so much that it could never recover.

It won't be easy. No battle worth fighting ever is.

This will be the story of the Revolution.

The war that turned your life around.

The fate of your future is in your hands.

Take back the freedom that is rightfully yours.

Join this revolution.

Win this war.

ABOUT THE AUTHOR

Jonathan Alexander-Scott is passionate about seeing people live a life free from debt and free from the trappings of financial insecurity. He lives in the UK with his wife and children. Jonathan loves educating and inspiring others to succeed and live the life of their dreams.

Learn more about Jonathan at:

        http://jonathanascott.wordpress.com

Or follow on Twitter: @scott_books.

Disclaimer

When addressing financial matters in this or any other book, J.A.Scott Publications, along with the author, have made every effort to ensure that the information we provide is accurate and up to date. However, we strongly advise that you consult a financial advisor if you are struggling with debt as individual circumstances vary and consequently no one case is identical to another.

The information in this book is provided as a guide but should not replace advice given to you by solicitors, financial advisors or any other professional.

If you are in the UK and are seriously struggling with debt then we would recommend that you contact CAP, an independent charity specialising in helping people escape debt.

Their website is http://www.capuk.org

www.ingramcontent.com/pod-product-compliance
Lightning Source LLC
Chambersburg PA
CBHW071749170526
45167CB00003B/991